Strange Stories from EXMOUTH

Tricia Gerrish

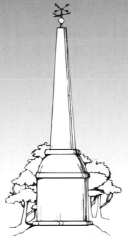

OBELISK PUBLICATIONS

Introduction

Whilst researching and writing features for BBC Radio Devon and Gemini AM Radio, I came across many unusual customs, superstitions and characters in the county of Devon's past about which I had previously been woefully ignorant. It was a double pleasure to share so many of them with listeners. The feedback received made it clear how many other people found them fascinating too. Every town in Devon has its share

of unusual tales, many involving ghosts or spirits. Some have no basis in fact. In others, a kernel of truth has probably been embroidered in the telling, through many generations. A third group appear to fit local and national history of their time, and enjoy the authentic ring of truth. Exmouth – an East Devon seaside resort which grew from its early *fisschar tounlet* – is no exception. Four of the seven stories which follow were recorded in well-known nineteenth century Devonshire sources. Each is pin-pointed geographically; several contain names associated with their period. Can we believe any to be entirely true? Gentle reader, the final decisions rest – with you!

Bell, Book and 'Baccy

The Church of St John in the Wilderness, formerly called St John the Baptist, still occupies its original site on the northern boundary of Exmouth. Until 1538 it was part of Polsloe Priory's estates, together with East Budleigh. It served as parish church of the Manor of Wythycombe Rawleigh in the days when Exmouth as we know it was divided between two manors: Wythycombe and Littleham. Herein lies the basis for our first strange story from Exmouth...

At the end of the fifteenth century the manor of Wythycombe Rawleigh, near Exmouth, belonged to one Sir Roger de Whalingham and included the already ancient church of St John in the Wilderness. Next door, so to speak, in Littleham, lived Sir Hugh de Creveldt, a man of German descent.

The two men hated each other. There were constant petty arguments between their tenants about cockle-raking areas, and gathering other shellfish in the Exe estuary. Sir Hugh claimed sole rights. Three periwinkles in his heraldic shield were, he stated, proof of this grant. Jealousy existed over their respective daughters, since Havise de Whalingham was adjudged Queen of Beauty of games held at nearby Newton Poppleford. Amabel de Creveldt had been virtually ignored. On one occasion when a shipwreck took place, the Wythycombe men got there first and secured a cargo of Genoese velvets for Sir Roger, whilst the de Creveldt men only salvaged sixteen jars of caviar – which caused Sir Hugh to employ some of his more choice German swear words.

Finally matters came to a head when the Lord of Littleham taunted Sir Roger over the family's skeletons: the ghosts from St John's in the Wilderness churchyard. It was believed that the de Whalingham family received nightly visits from these spectres, demanding musical requiems for their souls. The ghosts were said to join in the singing, and the resulting tunes carried on the wind towards the Exe valley. Sir Roger de Whalingham could not believe his ears. His neighbour was obviously no gentleman, to raise such a distressing matter. Finally, he uttered this curse: 'See to thyself de Creveldt, that when my spirit leaves this body, it visits thee not in thy fair domain of Littleham. It shall meet thee in thy walks, at thy table, and draw thy bed curtains, till thou prayest for the immortal minstrels of Wythycombe to sing their requiem to its disturbed and wandering spirit.' Not another word passed between the two men from that day forward.

Some years later, one stormy night in December, Sir Hugh de Creveldt dozed in his chair following a day's otter hunting. Three deep melancholy tolls of the bell of St John's Church roused him. He knew the sound of this bell, and its history. It had been christened by the Pope himself, and was one of only two bells in Europe believed to toll a knell for the departing spirit of members of its patron's family – without the need for mortal hand. The bells of Wythycombe, they say Spontaneous tell the fatal day.

Sir Hugh had been dreaming of his neighbour's threat when the bell tolled, and jumped to his feet hoping he was STILL dreaming. He waited, knowing that if the ringing continued beyond three strokes it was merely being tolled for one of Wythycombe's parishioners. It remained silent. He turned, to fling himself into his chair. Seated there was Sir Roger de Whalingham's ghost, clad in a velvet hat.

The spirit remained for about an hour, passed through the keyhole and left – only to return next day and three times daily for a month. Unlike a dose of medicine, these regular visits did nothing for de Creveldt's health. Mealtimes were worst; no matter what his cook provided it was instantly removed by the ghost and replaced with a plate of caviar. He ordered servants to sink the remainder of the consignment in the Exe. The ghost produced more. A gloom settled over Littleham, as the estate's owner pined away, almost to death.

In 1550, an Exeter ship, returning from Cadiz, anchored in the Exe. It was commanded by Captain Izaaks, known to Sir Hugh. On hearing the tale, the Captain offered to smoke out the ghost. 'But how?' asked de Creveldt. 'Ghosts are only smoke, air or vapour themselves.' 'Two of a trade may never agree,' replied the Captain, 'and I have in my cargo a weed which first came to Cadiz from America with friends of Christopher Columbus. It may be set alight in a tube, and will envelope the atmosphere in a closed room.' He explained that it is well known that spectres only breathe pure oxygen, without azote (an old name for nitrogen).

As soon as the apparition left, following its morning call, the Captain 'caulked' the room, as if it were the planking of a ship. Every keyhole, cranny or gap was sealed, to confine both the vapour and the spirit. Sir Roger's ghost entered as curlew pie was being served for supper, which was immediately replaced with a dish of caviar. The meal ended; the door was closed. Two tubes were produced, the Indian Weed, as it was called, lit, and the whole room filled with dense smoke. The spirit was soon invisible, but unearthly coughing and sneezes were heard. Captain Izaaks continued to smoke his pipe. At length, the ghost groaned: 'if thou wilt once open the door Sir Knight, I will haunt thee no more. Destroy me thou canst not. The poisonous vapour may affect my substance, but it cannot kill me.' A strange discussion then took place between haunter and haunted, and Sir Hugh de Creveldt was released from his curse.

He had, unfortunately, become addicted to the Indian Weed. In 1563, Sir Hugh was chased and mocked by spirits, on Woodbury Down. They prophesied that smoking would pursue him to his end, and that his sons would also be plagued by the addiction. He died within a week. Any connection with Sir Walter Raleigh? After the death of the last de Whalingham, his property fell into the hands of the Rawleigh family. It is said young Walter was so excited by the tale of the smoked-out ghost that one of his first adventuring acts was to bring back the Indian Weed from Virginia. He got the credit – or blame – for bringing it to England.

This tale claims to have come from descendents of Hugh de Creveldt. Its writer, in the *Western Miscellany* (1849), asserts that when attempts were later made to remove a crumbling St John's church tower, dreadful disasters befell those involved. A new chapel was built instead, in 'a more populous district', and the old church fell into decay. However, parish history researchers have discovered that the new chapel – later to become St John the Evangelist parish church in Withycombe Village itself – was petitioned and built before the dates relevant to this story. By the sixteenth century, St John in the Wilderness (a name probably not used until at least a century later) was only in occasional use for marriages – and burials. Its lonely location and neglected ivy-clad tower gave rise to today's name. They may also have lent substance to this tale.

Exmouth, Church of St. John in the Wilderness

The Apparition of Fontelautus Dennis

Apparitions were evidently commonplace in Georgian and early Victorian times. Was it something in the diet, or a lack of universal education? Exmouth boasts such an apparition, related in a book written by the Reverend Mr Dennis in 1826 concerning his son, and later retold in *Memorials of Exmouth*. Like many early-nineteenth century stories, it exhibits a touch of the gruesome…

Fontelautus, child of the Rev. Jonas Dennis of Bicton Street, died young. His father, who had decided the boy was inhabited by demons – probably suffering epileptic fits – arranged for exorcism. It is claimed this worked, but the boy's system had been so taxed that he died. (This sounds rather like our ancient test for a witch, where if she floated she was condemned and if she drowned she died anyway!)

On the following night, the remains of Fontelautus were moved to an attic, to prevent his grieving mother constantly inspecting the corpse. The coffin lid was secured until next morning, when it was to be re-opened to 'prevent condensation of putrescent exhalation' harming the bearers. The remaining Dennis children and their nursemaid had been sent to different sleeping quarters and the maid, lying in bed, heard Fontelautus' usual tone of voice, coaxing her to go in to him. This he had often done. She followed the voice – only half awake. It led her up the staircase to the attic, continuing to call her, so it seemed, from within the coffin. It was, of course, closed and fastened. That night his favourite sister Maria also heard him calling.

During the next two days this was repeated so vividly she expected to find her brother standing in the attic. His mother, in the dining room, heard the same sounds. Maria claimed to have seen her brother's hand stretching out of the attic window. 'See mother, quick,' she beckoned; 'see 'Lautus, he's alive!' As Mrs Dennis approached the hand withdrew. That night, as she lay grieving that Mr Dennis would not allow her to kiss her dead child's lips just once more, she heard a fluttering of wings. They seemed to touch her lips and fly round the room. Yet both door and window were shut and locked. What could have entered? She believed it was Fontelautus, possessed of angelic wings.

Fontelautus' day of burial arrived. Maria refused to help her four sisters carry his coffin, and returned from the funeral convinced he was being buried alive. She became almost insane; her father was forced to have his son exhumed and satisfy the girl's obsession. Luckily, for some reason Fontelautus had been buried in the garden – not in a local cemetery – making this procedure simpler.

A month later, the family cook admitted having seen a headless figure pass through her kitchen, from courtyard door to pantry, before vanishing. This preceded Fontelautus'

death by only a short period. The kitchen lay immediately below where the child had been decapitated, following death, for examination of the brain and skull 'to detect the extent of effused lymph'.

It is small wonder that by 1872, some 14 years before Mrs Hume Long converted it into a hospital, Belmont House in Bicton Street had the reputation among ordinary folk of being haunted. The site is occupied by Hatherleigh Cottages. It is difficult to believe, however, that, given the proximity of Holy Trinity churchyard, Fontelautus would really have been buried in a private garden in the nineteenth century, especially as his father was a man of the cloth.

The Mark of the Devil?

Most Devonians will know this story. Controversy still rages from time to time regarding its authenticity. Its recording in the *Exeter Flying Post, Woolmer's Exeter & Plymouth Gazette* and the *Illustrated London News* of 1855 should perhaps be taken with several pinches of salt, but you will never convince a Devon countryperson that Old Nick doesn't inhabit this county...

On the night of Thursday, February 8th 1855, it had been snowing heavily and the ground was frozen. These facts are essential – and convenient – to our tale. Inhabitants of East Devon, Teignbridge and Torbay (using today's administrative divisions for convenient location) awoke to a spine-chilling mystery. A huge, single line of prints had appeared in the snow overnight. Each measured 4 inches in length by 2 inches width, and they were between 8 and 12 inches apart. Even more terrifying, people said they resembled a hoof – perhaps even a cloven hoof. Could a donkey with one leg have made them? Could a donkey with one leg travel over 100 miles, for that was the distance discovered to have been traversed in one night – in a straight, single line? From Exmouth, the tracks passed through Bicton, East Budleigh, Woodbury, Clyst St George, Topsham and Lympstone, where they crossed a deeply frozen river Exe to continue South. Young Mr D'Urban of Countess Wear, nineteen years of age at the time, decided to plot their course from Totnes, and discovered that Torquay, Newton Abbot, Teignmouth and the Dawlish area up to Kenton had been similarly affected. The line was unbroken, as local people soon found out. When it reached a wall – even one as high as 14 feet – the line of prints continued as though the creature had gone over it.

House roofs were walked over, a drain pipe traversed inside. A shed wall was apparently walked through. There were prints underneath the lowest of shrubs. Snow, it is said, had been completely removed within each print back to soil level, as if sliced by a diamond – or branded with the hot irons of Hell! Surely this must be a visitation from the Devil. A clergyman at Lympstone felt obliged to preach to his congregation, seeking to allay their fears. 'Labourers, their wives and children, and old crones and trembling old men dreaded to stir out after sunset, or to go half a mile into lanes and byways … under the conviction that this was the Devil's walk, and no other.'

Once the *Illustrated London News* published its report on 24th February 1855 mayhem broke loose. Pressmen descended on Devon in droves. Local men accompanied them – armed, just in case. Theories began to flood in to newspaper offices. It was a practical joke. Marks were not made in one night. A story spread claiming Topsham's line of prints didn't appear until St Valentine's Eve. Was it a huge water bird, whose feet, released from a frozen river, were still surrounded by a block of ice? It would hardly have walked up buildings. A kangaroo had made them. Could a kangaroo have survived sub-zero temperatures over a long enough period to freeze a mile-wide river? Richard (later Sir Richard) Owen, an eminent palaeontologist, diagnosed the culprit from a cast as a badger. Various animals have been blamed during almost a century and a half. One of the best other suggestions was a mooring ring on knotted rope, trailed from a small balloon!

If the real explanation is natural, why did a pack of hounds, sent on the trails by some resourceful huntsmen, turn tail and rush from dense woodland howling, with coats standing up in fright? I think I'd rather believe in the Devil, even if he must have hopped, to make the story plausible, since Old Nick is supposed to have only ONE cloven hoof.

Future Imperfect

In an unnamed, but popular, periodical of 1847, claims *Memorials of Exmouth* (1872 edition), appeared a true story concerning the town of Exmouth, featuring a mysterious woman. The resort was referred throughout as Sunny Bay. However, every place named, and all the principal participants, can be matched with Exmouth at the relevant time. Perhaps avoidance of libel suits was in the editor's mind…

Sunny Bay (which WE will henceforth call Exmouth), within easy travel of Exeter, became a popular watering place in the late eighteenth century. First came the infirm and consumptive, to take the waters as recommended by royal physicians. Later, when the French Revolution prevented their annual trips to the continent, the upper crust and social climbers joined them. Hortense de Crespigny came to Exmouth to visit the Duc de Rohan's family. He'd found his doctor's advice to take the waters in the town helpful for consumption. Hortense, an 'exile for ever', decided Exmouth was as good a place as any to 'waste what remains to me of life'. The gossips were intrigued. Was she 25 – or 40? Where did she come from? She spoke five languages and seemed to have plenty of money.

A poor widowed lacemaker with several children succumbed to malignant fever. Two nurses attending her caught the disease, and she was left alone. Mlle de Crespigny decided to take over, and visited four times daily, paying Dr Luke of Exeter to attend at the crisis. The widow survived, blessing Hortense, and wishing her a long and happy life. Strangely, Mlle de C suggested she'd prefer the widow prayed that she be permitted to die. This piece of gossip spread, and Hortense became even more of a curiosity. She was seen to walk alone by the sea, saying the waves 'spoke' to her of the future; that they carried messages of the dead and distant, lost and loved. Her religious views were also suspect. Mrs Chapman, of the Globe Hotel (in what is now The Parade) called her a rank heretic. And then the self-righteous folk of Exmouth discovered that Hortense claimed to read the future. They were outraged.

Captain Carpenter's son was full of life, well-mannered, and destined for a brilliant future. 'We shall hear of him by the time he's 30,' people said. Mlle de C gazed at the lad and murmured that he'd not live to 20 – or even into his teens: 'He's doomed.' Six weeks or so later he decided to slide, via the balustrade in his home, from third floor to basement, and landed on his head. She had been proved correct.

The story came to the attention of Frances, Lady Nelson, resident on the Beacon. Lord Nelson had been a faithless husband, indifferent to his poor wife. However, she'd loved him and was desperate to know whether he had remembered her at the end. Lady Nelson spoke to the celebrated travel writer Marianna Starke, who lived at No. 11, about consulting Hortense to see if she could help. 'Consult that charlatan?' Ms Starke spluttered. 'She's probably a spy. I've been having her watched. Why does she never post her letters locally? She goes up to Exeter herself – a 20 mile round trip. Where there is mystery, there is iniquity.'

Viscountess Nelson couldn't leave matters as they stood. Perhaps Marianna Starke was simply jealous because she was getting less attention than normal since Mlle de C's arrival. She called at Hortense's cottage off The Parade. 'He did not mention you,' Hortense said, after some long thought, 'but he wrote a letter, eight days before going into action.' 'I never received it,' cried Lady Nelson. 'Are you surprised?' Mlle de C hinted that her visitor had enemies who'd ensured it got lost. She assured her that the tone of the letter had been 'kind and affectionate to the highest degree'. At which Lady Nelson felt obliged to express doubts.

'I'll just pass the remainder of my days in this little seaport. Its quiet calms me,' she resigned herself. 'Only a portion,' Hortense retorted. 'You will witness a frightful contest … at a revolution. It will be one of the most bitter times of your life, but not a hair on YOUR head will be harmed.' She refused to say another word, despite offers of money from Lady Nelson, who left and, at the time, told nobody, not even her son.

Next came the lost husband of Widow Hussey. This fisherman and his friend had been lost off Exmouth Bar. She was inconsolable, but eventually received another offer of marriage. Before setting the date, Widow Hussey decided to consult Hortense de Crespigny, just in case. 'Are you after two husbands?' asked Hortense. 'You'll be tried for bigamy.' Her first husband was still alive, according to Mlle de C, and would return to claim her.

Marianna Starke decided the 'supernatural must be cut down and the woman de Crespigny silenced.' She persuaded Dr Cave, a politician from North Street, to petition the magistrate, Mr Hull of Marpool Hall. He decided the gossips were encouraging Mlle de C and giving her the last laugh. 'But Hussey is dead, and it's unpardonable to upset his widow,' said Dr Cave. 'How do you know?' replied Mr Hull.

Next day Hortense de Crespigny had quit Exmouth. After a night burning papers, she'd left for Exeter at 4 a.m., taken the Post coach to Plymouth and vanished. Was she crazy? A spy in the pay of Lord Sidmouth – or agent of the French Government? She was seen in Downing Street, according to one local worthy, entering the Foreign Office dressed as a man!

When the Bourbon monarchy was restored in France, jails were emptied and privateers' captures released. Among them was the fisherman Hussey. Then came further revolution in France. And who was present? Lady Nelson, staying in a building searched by the gendarmerie in pursuit of one of the Polignac ministry. Her son Josiah was shot in the incident, almost in her presence, and other bullets killed young members of his family. Mlle de Crespigny's prophecies came true – many ironically showing a future that was imperfect. But who was she – and where did she go? To these questions there are as yet no answers.

Consider the following facts:

1. In 1830 Lady Nelson is well documented as resident at No. 6 The Beacon. She is

NELSON HOUSE
LADY NELSON, WIFE OF
ADMIRAL LORD HORATIO NELSON
RESIDED HERE DURING
THE YEARS 1803-1829

known to have ordered the exhumation and return of the bodies of her son and grandchildren from France. It is questionable whether the grandchildren were killed in unrest in Paris. They are usually referred to as having 'died young'. They arrived by sea late one evening. The bodies were taken by a resourceful Customs Officer to a partly-built house with crenellated roof on Exmouth's Morton Crescent for safety overnight, pending burial at Littleham Churchyard. Lady Nelson was herself interred there with them in 1831. For years the house was called Corpse Castle by local people. Nobody wanted to live there, except one old lady with several cats. Hence its alternative local name: Cats Castle.

2. Marianna Starke was a noted lady traveller and travel writer of repute, who occupied 11 The Beacon contemporary with Lady Nelson. She is recorded as having directed at least one exotic pageant in Exmouth, was noted for her direct manner, and died in Milan, en route back to Exmouth from Naples, in 1838.

3. The Hull family lived at Marpool Hall, and were Exmouth magistrates during the period of this story.

A Sixpenny Rail Warrant

A different but no less strange story features part of Exmouth's beach. The area near the Clock Tower, the Deer Leap (once a seawater bath house) and Exmouth Pavilion was often referred to as Little Beach early in the twentieth century. On the sands there, bathing machines jostled for space with boatmen and refreshment huts, one of which was run by Mrs Bessie (later known as Granny) Hunt…

Bessie started in business there, almost opposite where Bath Road meets the seafront, in 1901, with a canvas tent and a primus. Her rent was one shilling a year, paid to the Rolle Estate Office. When the Hon. Mark Rolle's lease was taken over by the local council in about 1904 everything changed. They decided to bring in bye-laws governing the use of Little Beach, with the effect of forcing all refreshment huts and pleasure boat owners off the foreshore. Bessie was offered an alternative pitch along at Orcombe, a mile or more away. She refused. It was too far from her home in Exmouth. She saw her predicament as part of a bigger problem.

The real reason for the changes, Bessie discovered, was a desire to privatise Little Beach. The council intended to lease sections of it to hotels on the nearby Beacon, and to keep the general public off. Children would not be allowed to use buckets and spades, lest they dug a pit.

There was a streak of the radical in Mrs Hunt, who argued that, since high 'spring' tides came up the sands beyond her refresh-

ment booth, nobody was entitled to own Little Beach. The spot on which she worked was No Man's – unclaimed land. Neither police nor council had authority over it. Arguments dragged on and became heated.

On a memorable day – June 29th 1906 – having been given notice, with other beach vendors Mrs Fowler and Mrs Holden, that the U.D.C. had obtained judgement against her, Bessie was in her usual spot. Police Sergeant Staddon, accompanied by the Borough Surveyor, arrived to enforce their order. The other two women shifted onto the sea wall, leaving Bessie to face authority alone. Her first reaction was to pour hot water on the unwanted visitors. When this was ineffective, she lay down on her stall's counter and dared them to arrest her, in an area where they 'had no authority'.

The siege continued until evening. Eventually she left the beach, was apprehended in the town and taken to Exeter Gaol on remand. Despite the worries of a husband, blinded just after their last son was born in 1902, and her family responsibilities, Mrs Hunt continued to battle from prison. She petitioned the Local Government Board in Whitehall, through her M.P. A furore rapidly developed in Exmouth, councillors finding their viewpoint in the minority. Visitors came down from London to listen to Bessie's contention regarding Little Beach. At the end of 21 days, the Board 'found' for Mrs Hunt, and awarded her a spot on the beach for life. Bessie was released and given a rail warrant, value sixpence, from Queen Street station (now Exeter Central) to Exmouth. She disdained their free ticket, paid the sixpence herself, and kept the warrant as proof of the outcome.

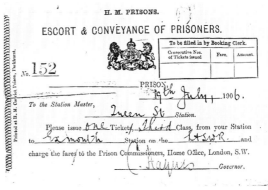

She was soon back in business on Little Beach, although with a higher rent. Granny Hunt's canvas tent was replaced by a wooden hut. She was the first to have water piped to her premises. Every drop had formerly been carried from a standpipe on the far side of the promenade. The rent was now £10 per annum (it would eventually reach £100) and she told the council that she expected some facilities for the money. A gas supply later followed.

A day's work for Granny Hunt was long and arduous. She opened by 6 a.m., doing some of her best trade between then and 9 o'clock. Visitors staying in hotels and guesthouses, before the days of kettles in the room and teamakers, came out for an early stroll and a freshly brewed cup of tea at Number 1 Hut. She never sold a pot of tea; jugs or cups were the rule, and she poured every one herself. Commercial travellers found their way to Granny's hut, usually sending a postcard announcing their impending arrival. On one occasion, a postcard bore not a traveller's message but a hot racing tip from a daughter working in Birmingham. (Bessie and husband Albert loved a flutter.) Albert took it, as was his habit, to be read out by the barber who shaved him, and the local bookmaker's runner enjoyed a brisk trade. The horse won! Mrs Hunt once used her refreshment hut to hide the runner from a local constable. His satchel, in a newspaper parcel given to her granddaughter as scraps, changed hands under the

policeman's nose. Bessie gave up the lease of Number 1 Hut around 1937, believing another war was inevitable, and that the beach would be commandeered. She moved along the promenade to the new outdoor swimming pool, and ran a refreshment hut there – until the age of 80, when she decided she had earned her retirement.

Bessie Hunt's story cannot be disputed. A jug from 'Number 1 Hut' may be seen in Exmouth Museum, who also have the original rail warrant issued by HM Prisons, dated 19th July 1906. Granny Hunt hated being photographed, so I am fortunate to have a somewhat faded picture of her, with a young friend, in the wooden hut on Little Beach. Note the jugs hanging up inside. Newspaper reports too back up this strange tale. I am most grateful to her granddaughter Mrs Kitty Mantle for filling in the details.

The Phantom Messenger

Another spirit story featured as recently as the 1940s in material on haunted England. Several local people have told me versions…

A young man, staying in Exmouth in the mid-nineteenth century, woke one night at precisely twelve of the clock. He felt compelled to get up, dress and leave his place of lodging. He wasn't about to rob anyone, dig up corpses for medical research, set off on a midnight fishing trip – or even keep a romantic assignation. His compulsion – the voice in his head which wouldn't be silenced – told him to go down to the ferry. This was, in those days, a dark and eerie place at night, situated as it would have been on The Point, or landspit, jutting out into the Exe estuary, and overshadowed by the remains of Exmouth's windmill. Cold logic told him there would be no boat available at this hour. The ferryman, who then lived at Starcross, was certain to be asleep in bed. Yet he could not help himself. He HAD to go. Imagine his amazement when he squelched down over the mud and discarded cockle and mussel shells, to discover a boat ready and waiting for a journey. 'How come?' he gratefully asked the ferryman. 'Someone battered on my door and called out that a passenger was waiting on the Exmouth side,' he answered. 'And that it was urgent. They'd gone by the time I'd got the latch off.'

The pair reached Starcross and the young man paid his dues. His feet seemed to have decided the next move. They carried him inexorably towards the railway station, where he took an early train to Exeter – with the milk, no doubt.

Once in this city, the man wandered its streets somewhat aimlessly, still puzzling why he was there. Eventually, his stomach answered for him, and he entered a nearby hotel for some breakfast. All was bustle and hurry. He asked a waiter if Exeter was always like this. 'Why no sir,' he said. 'You must be a stranger to town, or you'd know that the Assizes are in session. It's always like this here when the big courts sit.'

As he was there – and still had no real idea why – our Exmouth lodger decided to while away an hour or two finding out what villains Devon had bred recently. He followed the crowds to the Castle, as it was known, and chose – he thought at random – which court to visit first. A carpenter was on trial there for murder.

It was a sad tale, involving this previously-honest artisan. All the poor man could do was assert his innocence, and offer an alibi for the time when the offence had been committed. An alibi for which there was, alas, no corroboration. On the day in question he had been working at a big house several miles from the scene of crime. Unfortunately, the job had deliberately been timed to coincide with the family who owned it being away. They had, as was common in the mid-nineteenth century, taken most of their staff with them – and given the rest a holiday (without pay, no doubt). 'Very convenient,' the prosecuting counsel scoffed. 'Nobody can say he wasn't there – but equally, there's not a soul to say he was. Guilty, without a shadow of doubt.' 'There's only one man as can prove my innocence, m'lord,' said the poor man, 'but I don't know where to find him.' A young friend of the householder had called on that day, on the off-chance for a visit, he told the judge, and could therefore have vouched for the carpenter's presence. He particularly remembered the young man's visit, the accused continued, as he had lent him his pencil to make entries in a notebook he carried. (Knowing how most people behave when you lend them a biro nowadays, the carpenter was unlikely to have had it returned.)

At last! The young man staying at Exmouth knew why he'd been dragged from his bed. He knew why he'd taken an early train, and why he was in this particular courtroom on this particular day. HE was the man who had visited the house – the man who had borrowed the carpenter's pencil. From an inside pocket, he was able to produce the all-important notebook, in which he had made several entries. They clearly referred to matters involving the house where the accused claimed to have been working when murder was committed elsewhere, and – since the young man was careful and methodical – were even dated. After a shamefaced search, eyewitnesses said, he held up the pencil stub with which they were written. The case against the carpenter collapsed. He left the court a free and fortunate man, thanking his young deliverer with tears in his eyes.

The inference of this story is that both the young man staying in Exmouth and the ferryman were guided by spirits. Some raconteurs have even pinpointed the big house

as Powderham Castle (seat of the Earls of Devonshire). Written and corroborative detail are lacking for 'The Phantom Messenger'. I have added the details of the Exmouth to Starcross ferry as it would have been in the mid-nineteenth century myself, to make this version more atmospheric. Perhaps, like many 'strange stories' in Devon, spirits of a different nature, and a pot or two of the local cider, have gradually added colour in the telling. One question remains tantalisingly unanswered in this story: did the police ever apprehend the real villain?

A Curious Habit in South Street

The last strange story is, appropriately, up-to-date. The history of South Street in Exmouth is also the history of the town's working classes. A medical officer's report in 1849 makes it clear disease and poverty were constant companions. South Street was in an area where large dung heaps and open sewers were common. It is hardly surprising that this part of Exmouth was badly affected by the cholera epidemic of 1833. Many harrowing tales could be told by the older properties behind what is now the Magnolia Shopping Centre car park. Perhaps this final 'strange story' – a modern apparition – relates to one of these. Maybe it/she was seeking to attract the occupants' attention…

No. 7 South Street is part of a run of houses where old flagstones and other features speak of a fairly lengthy history. By repute, it was once part of a larger property, possibly a farm. In the late 1990s it was rented to a young mother whose two-year-old daughter – bright, chatty and very aware – wasted no time in getting to know the place, soon discovering an extra occupant. At first the mother suspected her daughter's chat about a 'lady' was childhood imagination – until a 'nun' was mentioned, several times. The little girl even placed a teatowel over her head, held close around the face: 'like my nun'. To the mother's knowledge, the word and persona were unfamiliar to her young daughter. On one occasion, the child pointed to several nuns, in old-style full-length habits and white wimples, on the television set. 'There's my nun.' Mother began to wonder.

A two-level room, currently the bathroom and separate toilet, with a large window in the latter – and small arrow-slit overlooking an old courtyard backing onto Fore Street and Pound Street in the former – was focal point for the phantom nun's visits.

'It's the nun, Mummy, d'you want to talk?' said the small girl, holding out a showerhead attached to the bath's mixer taps one bathtime. In retrospect Grandma – who related this story, as her daughter still finds it painful to discuss – wishes she had done so. If only to find out whether someone was on the other end of the line!

Others visiting the house bear witness to the child's comments about her nun, who seems only to have wished friendship and contact with a young person. She never revealed herself to anyone else, although on one occasion at least three people were sitting on a downstairs sofa when a sudden wind blew. 'Oh, here's my nun,' said the little girl. The others were quite 'spooked' by it. It might still have been possible to feel the South Street Nun's presence nowadays, but for one telling event – and its consequences.

At around lunchtime one day, in broad daylight, the child's mother decided to run a bath. Bending over the mixer taps checking water temperature she realised that reflected in them were: not one, but two images. The first she recognised as a distortion of her own face; the other, looking over her shoulder, was – the mother had no doubt – the nun. There was nobody else in the house. Unlike her child, the mother was unable to cope with confirmation of this additional presence. She rang her mother, who came to South Street, entered the bathroom and told the nun off for bothering her daughter. She remembers a 'twisting' feeling in her abdomen as she uttered the words – later wondering if their poltergeist had finally turned vindictive.

Her suggestion to seek advice from the church led, next day, to the office of Exmouth's Roman Catholic parish church in Raddenstile Lane. A priest agreed to call later. He entered the bathroom at No. 7 South Street, and immediately commented that he understood the problem – as if he too had sensed a presence or poltergeist. As the child had never experienced nightmares, or distress, and given the single instance of possible spite, he suggested gentle exorcism in the form of blessing. The family gladly left him to perform this – alone. Although other children (believed by the family to be the attraction or catalyst for the poltergeist) have stayed or lived at No. 7, nobody has since seen, heard or sensed the nun's ghostly presence there...

I have tried to pinpoint the location of this story against known facts about Exmouth before the Second World War bombing altered its town centre, to see whether a convent or similar building was nearby. Perhaps nuns from the convent in Boarden Barn would have nursed the poor in times of epidemic – for little or no charge. We know South Street was an unhealthy area 150 years or more ago. Could St Margaret's Chapel (Fore Street/Chapel Street) have any connection? Nothing can be proved.

There is, however, a 'sting in the tail' – or rather 'tale' – of our last strange story from Exmouth. Since the exorcism in South Street, a known psychic from the Fore Street area has sensed the presence (without prior knowledge of this tale, I hasten to add) of a nun on the corner of Fore and South Streets. She is in some distress, says the psychic, being unable to enter South Street. The small child's grandmother hopes it is not the same spirit, or she will feel guilty for having prevented her being at rest. If not, what was the attraction of this area for ghostly Brides of Christ in the late 1990s?